Jane Goodall:
Friend of the Apes

written by Mary Lindeen   illustrated by Marty Martinez

Content Consultant:
Randall Susman, Professor of Anatomical Sciences
School of Medicine, Stony Brook University

magic
wagon

visit us at www.abdopublishing.com

Published by Magic Wagon, a division of the ABDO Publishing Group, 8000 West 78th Street, Edina, Minnesota 55439. Copyright © 2009 by Abdo Consulting Group, Inc. International copyrights reserved in all countries. All rights reserved. No part of this book may be reproduced in any form without written permission from the publisher.

Looking Glass Library™ is a trademark and logo of Magic Wagon.

Printed in the United States.

Text by Mary Lindeen
Illustrations by Marty Martinez
Edited by Nadia Higgins
Interior layout and design by Emily Love
Cover design by Emily Love

Library of Congress Cataloging-in-Publication Data

Lindeen, Mary.
  Jane Goodall : friend of the apes / by Mary Lindeen ; illustrated by Marty Martinez.
    p. cm. — (Beginner biographies)
  Includes index.
  ISBN 978-1-60270-249-3
  1. Goodall, Jane, 1934—Juvenile literature. 2. Primatologists—England—Biography—Juvenile literature. 3. Women primatologists—England—Biography—Juvenile literature. 4. Chimpanzees—Tanzania—Gombe Stream National Park—Juvenile literature. I. Martinez, Marty, ill. II. Title.
  QL31.G58L55 2009
  590.92—dc22
  [B]
                              2008002895

Table of Contents

The Early Years

Jane Goodall was born in London, England, on April 3, 1934. As a little girl, she loved learning about animals. She watched them in her backyard. She read books about them. She dreamed about going to Africa to see the interesting animals that lived there.

When she was a teenager, Jane went to school to become a secretary. But she never stopped thinking about Africa.

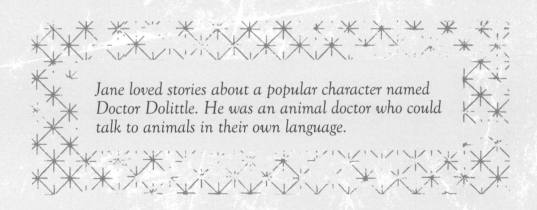

Jane loved stories about a popular character named Doctor Dolittle. He was an animal doctor who could talk to animals in their own language.

Jane daydreamed about wild animals when she was a girl.

Moving to Africa

When Goodall was 22, a friend who lived in Africa invited her for a visit. Goodall worked as a waitress to save money to make the trip. Then she quit her job. She sailed for Kenya, a country in eastern Africa.

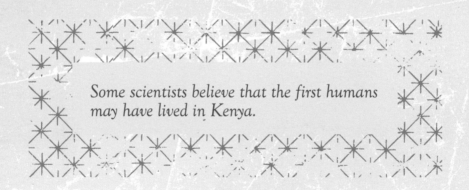

Some scientists believe that the first humans may have lived in Kenya.

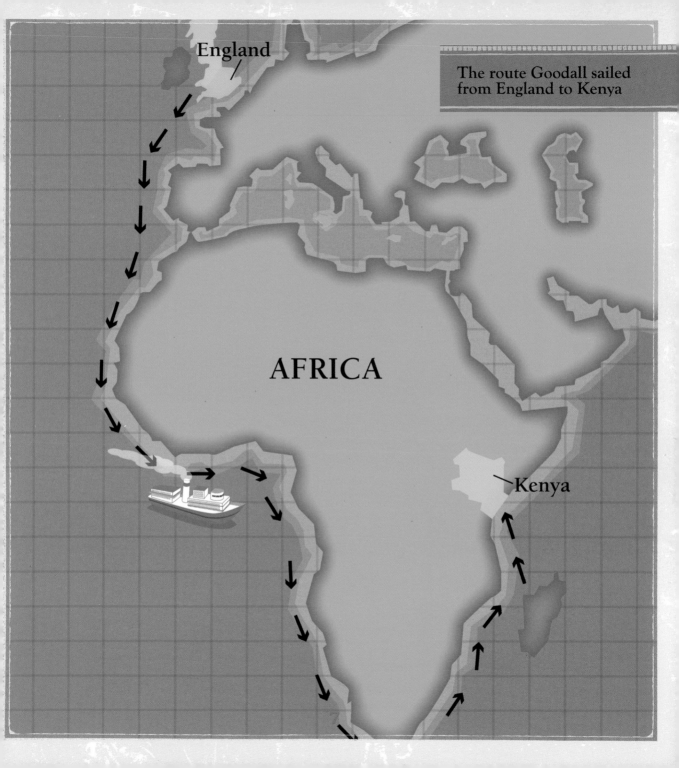

England

The route Goodall sailed
from England to Kenya

AFRICA

Kenya

Goodall worked side by side with Dr. Louis Leakey.

AFRICAN EXHIBIT

In Kenya, Goodall started working at a museum. She learned a lot about African animals. She impressed Dr. Louis Leakey, the museum's director. He invited Goodall to help him look for fossils in the grasslands of East Africa.

Goodall loved watching wild animals living on their own.

Digging for Fossils

Dr. Leakey and his team of scientists spent three months looking for fossils. The weather was hot and dry, and the work was tiring. But Goodall didn't mind. The grasslands were home to herds of zebras and many other animals. She loved watching the wildlife there.

After the fossil dig, Goodall went back to work at the museum. She thought about all the wild animals she had seen. She hoped she could work with those animals someday.

Living with Chimpanzees

Goodall's wish soon came true. Dr. Leakey asked her to study chimpanzees. He believed that learning more about chimpanzees, or chimps, would tell scientists more about the first humans. Whoever took the job would have to live in the forest for several years. And the person would have to love animals. Goodall was perfect for the job!

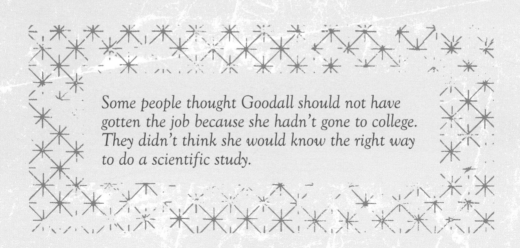

Some people thought Goodall should not have gotten the job because she hadn't gone to college. They didn't think she would know the right way to do a scientific study.

Goodall packed for her move to the forest.

13

In 1960, Goodall went to live in the Gombe Stream Chimpanzee Reserve. Her mother, Vanne, came along. This way, Goodall would not be all alone in the wilderness.

At first, the chimps did not trust Goodall. They would not come near her. But Goodall patiently kept watching and waiting. After a while, the chimps let her come quite close.

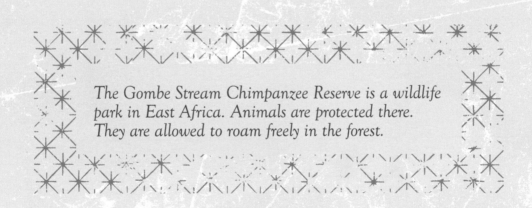

The Gombe Stream Chimpanzee Reserve is a wildlife park in East Africa. Animals are protected there. They are allowed to roam freely in the forest.

Goodall and her mother often enjoyed campfires at the Gombe reserve.

Goodall was able to watch
wild chimpanzees up close.

Learning about Chimpanzees

Goodall studied the chimpanzees at Gombe for years. She got to know them very well. She even gave many of them names. She learned that chimpanzees and humans are alike in many ways.

She discovered that chimps hold hands and hug. She watched mother chimps take care of their babies. The mothers carried and played with their babies. Even older brother and sister chimps liked to help take care of the babies. Like humans, baby chimps learn a lot from their family members.

Chimpanzees play and make tools.

Goodall learned that young chimps like to play together. They wrestle and swing from treetops. This helps the chimps practice skills they will need when they are older.

Goodall also learned facts about chimpanzees that no one knew. She found out that chimps hunt together and eat meat. They make simple tools and use them to get food. She also discovered that chimps fight and sometimes kill each other. She even saw grown-up chimps kill baby chimps.

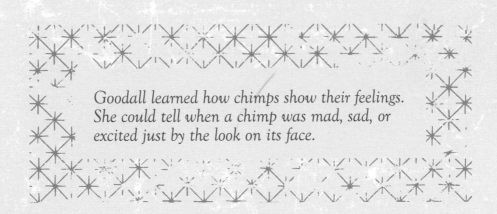

Goodall learned how chimps show their feelings. She could tell when a chimp was mad, sad, or excited just by the look on its face.

Marriage and Motherhood

In 1962, a photographer named Hugo van Lawick arrived at Jane's camp. He came to take pictures of Goodall and the chimps. He and Goodall ended up falling in love. They got married and had a son named Hugo.

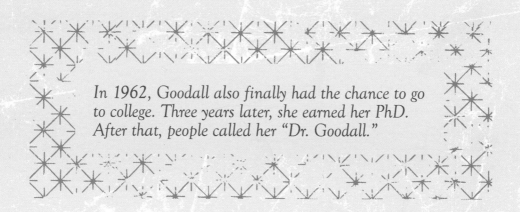

In 1962, Goodall also finally had the chance to go to college. Three years later, she earned her PhD. After that, people called her "Dr. Goodall."

Van Lawick also photographed
Goodall and their son, Hugo.

21

In 1974, Goodall and her husband got a divorce. The next year, she married Derek Bryceson, a park director in Africa. Around that same time, Goodall began to travel more. She wanted to talk to people about saving animals.

Goodall taught others how to save and protect wild animals.

Helping Others Study and Learn

In 1977, she started the Jane Goodall Institute. The group helps pay for research on animals. It also sets up programs worldwide to help protect animals.

In 1980, Goodall's husband, Derek, died of cancer. She was very sad, but her work helped her feel better.

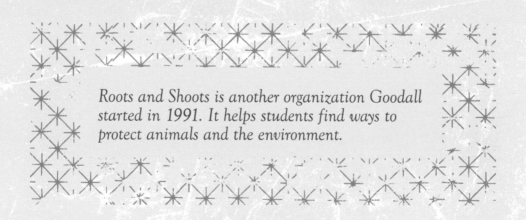

Roots and Shoots is another organization Goodall started in 1991. It helps students find ways to protect animals and the environment.

Members of Roots and Shoots plant trees and do other things to help the environment.

25

Traveling the World

Over the years, Goodall has been given many awards for her work. In 2002, the United Nations named her a "Messenger of Peace." Goodall has also written many books and magazine articles. She has been a visiting teacher at many colleges and universities. She has also been in many television programs and movies.

Goodall accepted her award from Kofi Annan, the secretary-general of the United Nations.

Goodall watches a chimpanzee at Gombe.

Today, Goodall still visits the chimpanzees in Gombe for a few weeks every year. She spends most of her time traveling around the world. She asks people to work together to protect animals and the world that we share with them.

FUN FACTS

✦ On Jane's second birthday, her father gave her a toy chimpanzee. She named him Jubilee. Today, the favorite toy sits on her dresser in her home in England.

✦ These are some of the names Goodall gave the chimps at Gombe: Flo, Flint, Frodo, Gilka, Goliath, Mike, Passion, Pom, and Otta.

✦ The president of Tanzania gave Goodall the Kilimanjaro Medal. It was the first time that medal had ever been given to someone who was not a citizen of that country.

TIMELINE

1934   Goodall was born on April 3.

1952   Goodall left school and began working.

1957   Goodall moved to Kenya.

1960   Goodall and her mother arrived at the Gombe Stream Chimpanzee Reserve.

1965   Goodall earned her PhD.

1977   Goodall founded the Jane Goodall Institute.

1991   Goodall founded the Roots and Shoots organization.

2002   Goodall was named a "Messenger of Peace" by the United Nations.

GLOSSARY

Africa—a large continent near Europe and Asia.

chimpanzee—a small ape with dark fur that comes from Africa.

divorce—the ending of a marriage.

fossil—the hardened remains of an animal or plant that lived millions of years ago.

reserve—a protected wilderness area where wild animals can live safely.

United Nations—an organization of countries that tries to spread world peace.

LEARN MORE

At the Library

Goodall, Jane. *The Chimpanzees I Love: Saving Their World and Ours*. New York: Scholastic, 2001.

Kendall, Martha E. *For the Love of Chimps: The Jane Goodall Story*. Logan, IA: Perfection Learning, 2005.

Kittinger, Jo S. *Jane Goodall*. New York: Children's Press, 2005.

On the Web

To learn more about Jane Goodall, visit ABDO Publishing Company on the World Wide Web at **www.abdopublishing.com**. Web sites about Goodall are featured on our Book Links page. These links are routinely monitored and updated to provide the most current information available.

INDEX